D1600385

The Aquinas Lecture, 1968

THE SUBJECT

Under the Auspices of the
Wisconsin-Alpha Chapter of Phi Sigma Tau

By

BERNARD LONERGAN, S.J., S.T.D.

MARQUETTE UNIVERSITY PRESS
MILWAUKEE
1968

Fourth Printing 1982

ISBN 0-87462-133-X

Library of Congress Catalog Number 68-22238

PRINTED
IN
U.S.A.

Prefatory

The Wisconsin-Alpha Chapter of Phi Sigma Tau, The National Honor Society for Philosophy at Marquette University, each year invites a scholar to deliver a lecture in honor of St. Thomas Aquinas whose feast day is March 7. These lectures are customarily given on the first or second Sunday of March.

The 1968 Aquinas Lecture *The Subject* was delivered on March 3 in the Peter A. Brooks Memorial Union by Rev. Bernard Lonergan, S.J., professor of Dogmatic Theology, Regis College (Ontario) and Gregorian University (Rome).

Fr. Lonergan was born in Buckingham, Quebec, on December 17, 1904. He earned the B.A. at the University of London in 1930, the S.T.D. at the Gregorian University in 1940. He taught theology at L'Immaculée Conception (Montreal) from 1940-1947. From that date until 1953 he was professor of Dogmatic Theology at the Jesuit Seminary (Toronto) and for the next twelve years held the same position at the Gregorian University. In 1965 he returned to Canada and at present is at Regis College, Ontario.

Fr. Lonergan's interest in theology as a kind of knowledge turned him towards a philosophical analysis of knowledge. The result of this inquiry is his important book, *Insight: A Study of Human Understanding*. In 1947 he received the Cardinal Spellman Award for outstanding scholarship in sacred theology.

Fr. Lonergan's publications include: *De Constitutione Christi*, Rome: Pontificia Universitas, 1956 (now in 4th printing); *Insight*, London, New York: Longmans, Green, 1957; *De Deo Trino*, 2 vols., Rome: Pontificia Universitas, 1964; *Collection*, New York: Herder and Herder, 1967; *Verbum, Word and Idea in Aquinas*, Notre Dame: Notre Dame University Press, 1967; articles in many philosophical and theological journals.

To these publications Phi Sigma Tau is pleased to add: *The Subject*.

The Subject

There is a sense in which it may be said that each of us lives in a world of his own. That world usually is a bounded world, and its boundary is fixed by the range of our interests and our knowledge. There are things that exist, that are known to other men, but about them I know nothing at all. There are objects of interest that concern other men, but about them I could not care less. So the extent of our knowledge and the reach of our interests fix a horizon. Within that horizon we are confined.

Such confinement may result from the historical tradition within which we are born, from the limitations of the social milieu in which we were brought up, from our individual psychological aptitudes, efforts, misadventures. But besides specifically historical, social, and psychological determinants of subjects and their horizons, there also are philosophic factors, and to a consideration of such factors the present occasion invites us.

The Neglected Subject

In contemporary philosophy there is a great emphasis on the subject, and this emphasis may easily be traced to the influence of Hegel, Kierkegaard, Nietzsche, Heidegger, Buber.[1] This fact, however, points to a previous period of neglect, and it may not be amiss to advert to the causes of such neglect, if only to make sure that they are no longer operative in our own thinking.

A first cause, then, is the objectivity of truth. The criterion, I believe, by which we arrive at the truth is a virtually unconditioned.[2] But an unconditioned has no conditions. A subject may be needed to arrive at truth but, once truth is attained, one is beyond the subject and one has reached a realm that is non-spatial, atemporal, impersonal. Whatever is true at any time or place, can be contradicted only by falsity. No one can gainsay it, unless he is mistaken and errs.

Such is the objectivity of truth. But do not be fascinated by it. Intentionally it is independent of the subject, but ontologically it resides only in the subject: *veritas formaliter est in solo iudicio*. Intentionally it goes completely beyond the subject, yet it does so only because ontologically the subject is capable of an intentional self-transcendence, of going beyond what he feels, what he imagines, what he thinks, what seems to him, to something utterly different, to what is so. Moreover, before the subject can attain the self-transcendence of truth, there is the slow and laborious process of conception, gestation, parturition. But teaching and learning, investigating, coming to understand, marshalling and weighing the evidence, these are not independent of the subject, of times and places, of psychological, social, historical conditions. The fruit of truth must grow and mature on the tree of the subject, before it can be plucked and placed in its absolute realm.

It remains that one can be fascinated by the objectivity of truth, that one can so emphasize objective truth as to disregard or undermine the very conditions of its emergence and existence. In fact, if at the present time among Catholics there is discerned a widespread alienation from the dogmas of faith, this is not unconnected with a previous one-sidedness that so insisted on the objectivity of truth as to leave subjects and their needs out of account.

Symptomatic of such one-sidedness was the difficulty experienced by theologians from the days of Suarez, de Lugo, and Bañez, when confronted with the syllogism: What God has revealed is true. God has revealed the mysteries of faith. Therefore, the mysteries of faith are true.[3] There is, perhaps, no need for me to explain why this syllogism was embarrassing, for it implied that the mysteries of faith were demonstrable conclusions. But the point I wish to make is that the syllogism contains an unnoticed fallacy, and the fallacy turns on an exaggerated view of the objectivity of truth. If one recalls that truth exists formally only in judgments and that judgments exist only in the mind, then the fallacy is easily pinned down. What God

reveals is a truth in the mind of God and
in the minds of believers, but it is not a
truth in the minds of non-believers; and
to conclude that the mysteries of faith are
truths in the mind of God or in the minds
of believers in no way suggests that the
mysteries are demonstrable. But this simple
way out seems to have been missed by the
theologians. They seem to have thought
of truth as so objective as to get along
without minds. Nor does such thinking
seem to have been confined to theoretical
accounts of the act of faith. The same in-
sistence on objective truth and the same
neglect of its subjective conditions in-
formed the old catechetics, which the new
catechetics is replacing, and the old censor-
ship, which insisted on true propositions
and little understood the need to respect
the dynamics of the advance toward truth.

Another source of neglect of the subject is to be found remotely in the Aristotelian notion of science, propounded in the
Posterior Analytics, and proximately in the
rationalist notion of pure reason. When
scientific and philosophic conclusions fol-

low necessarily from premises that are self-evident, then the road to science and to philosophy is not straight and narrow but broad and easy. There is no need to be concerned with the subject. No matter who he is, no matter what his interests, almost no matter how cursory his attention, he can hardly fail to grasp what is self-evident and, having grasped it, he can hardly fail to draw conclusions that are necessary. On such assumptions everything is black or white. If one happens to have opinions, one will have to defend them as self-evident or demonstrable. If one begins to doubt, one is likely to end up a complete skeptic. There is no need for concern with the subject, for the maieutic art of a Socrates, for intellectual conversion, for open-mindedness, striving, humility, perseverance.

A third source of neglect of the subject is the metaphysical account of the soul. As plants and animals, so men have souls. As in plants and animals, so in men the soul is the first act of an organic body. Still the souls of plants differ essentially from the souls of animals, and the souls of both differ essentially from the souls of men. To discern these differences we must turn from the soul to its potencies, habits, acts, objects. Through the objects we know the acts, through the acts we know the habits, through the habits we know the potencies, and through the potencies we know the essence of the soul. The study of the soul, then, is totally objective. One and the same method is applied to study of plants, animals, and men. The results are completely universal. We have souls whether we are awake or asleep, saints or sinners, geniuses or imbeciles.

The study of the subject is quite different, for it is the study of oneself inasmuch as one is conscious. It prescinds from the soul, its essence, its potencies, its habits, for none of these are given in consciousness. It attends to operations and to their center and source which is the self. It discerns the different levels of consciousness, the consciousness of the dream, of the waking subject, of the intelligently inquiring subject, of the rationally reflecting subject, of the responsibly deliberating subject. It examines the different operations on the several levels and their relations to one another.

Subject and soul, then, are two quite different topics. To know one does not exclude the other in any way. But it very easily happens that the study of the soul leaves one with the feeling that one has no need to study the subject and, to that extent, leads to a neglect of the subject.[4]

The Truncated Subject

The neglected subject does not know himself. The truncated subject not only does not know himself but also is unaware of his ignorance and so, in one way or another, concludes that what he does not know does not exist. Commonly enough the palpable facts of sensation and speech are admitted. Commonly also there is recognized the difference between sleeping and waking. But if universal, daytime somnambulism is not upheld, behaviorists would pay no attention to the inner workings of the subject; logical positivists would confine meaning to sensible data and the structures of mathematical logic; pragmatists would divert our attention to action and results.

But there are less gross procedures. One can accept an apparently reasonable rule of acknowledging what is certain and disregarding what is controverted. Almost inevitably this will lead to an oversight of insight. For it is easy enough to be certain about concepts; their existence can be inferred from linguistic usage and from scientific generality. But it is only by close attention to the data of consciousness that one can discover insights, acts of understanding with the triple role of responding to inquiry, grasping intelligible form in sensible representations, and grounding the formation of concepts. So complex a matter will never be noticed as long as the subject is neglected, and so there arises conceptualism: a strong affirmation of concepts, and a skeptical disregard of insights. As insights fulfil three functions, so conceptualism has three basic defects.

A first defect is an anti-historical immobilism. Human understanding develops and, as it develops, it expresses itself in ever more precise and accurate concepts, hypotheses, theories, systems. But conceptualism, as it disregards insight, so it cannot account for the development of concepts. Of themselves, concepts are immobile. They ever remain just what they are defined to mean. They are abstract and so stand outside the spatio-temporal world of change. What does change, is human understanding and, when understanding changes or develops, then defining changes or develops. So it is that, while concepts do not change on their own, still they are changed as the mind that forms them changes.

A second defect of conceptualism is an excessive abstractness. For the generalities of our knowledge are related to concrete reality in two distinct manners. There is the relation of the universal to the particular, of *man* to *this man*, of *circle* to *this circle*. There is also the far more important relation of the intelligible to the sensible,

of the unity or pattern grasped by insight
to the data in which the unity or pattern
is grasped. Now this second relation, which
parallels the relation of form to matter, is
far more intimate than the first. The universal abstracts from the particular, but the
intelligibility, grasped by insight, is immanent in the sensible and, when the sensible datum, image, symbol, is removed, the
insight vanishes. But conceptualism ignores
human understanding and so it overlooks
the concrete mode of understanding that
grasps intelligibility in the sensible itself. It
is confined to a world of abstract universals,
and its only link with the concrete is the
relation of universal to particular.

A third defect of conceptualism has to
do with the notion of being. Conceptual-
ists have no difficulty in discovering a concept of being, indeed, in finding it implicit
in every positive concept. But they think
of it as an abstraction, as the most abstract
of all abstractions, least in connotation and
greatest in denotation. In fact, the notion
of being is not abstract but concrete. It intends everything about everything. It pre-

scinds from nothing whatever. But to advert to this clearly and distinctly, one must note not only that concepts express acts of understanding but also that both acts of understanding and concepts respond to questions. The notion of being first appears in questioning. Being is the unknown that questioning intends to know, that answers partially reveal, that further questioning presses on to know more fully. The notion of being, then, is essentially dynamic, proleptic, an anticipation of the entirety, the concreteness, the totality, that we ever intend and since our knowledge is finite never reach.

The neglected subject, then, leads to the truncated subject, to the subject that does not know himself and so unduly impoverishes his account of human knowledge. He condemns himself to an antihistorical immobilism, to an excessively jejune conjunction between abstract concepts and sensible presentations, and to ignorance of the proleptic and utterly concrete character of the notion of being.

The Immanentist Subject

The subject is within but he does not remain totally within. His knowing involves an intentional self-transcendence. But while his knowing does so, he has to know his knowing to know that it does so. Such knowledge is denied the neglected and the truncated subject and so we come to the merely immanent subject.

The key to doctrines of immanence is an inadequate notion of objectivity. Human knowing is a compound of many operations of different kinds. It follows that the objectivity of human knowing is not some single uniform property but once more a compound of quite different properties found in quite different kinds of operation.[5] There is an experiential objectivity in the givenness of the data of sense and of the data of consciousness. But such experiential objectivity is not the one and only ingredient in the objectivity of human knowing. The process of inquiry, investigation, reflection, coming to judge is governed throughout by the exigences of human intelligence and human reasonableness; it is these exi-

gences that, in part, are formulated in logics
and methodologies; and they are in their
own way no less decisive than experiential
objectivity in the genesis and progress of
human knowing. Finally, there is a third,
terminal, or absolute type of objectivity,
that comes to the fore when we judge, when
we distinguish sharply between what we
feel, what we imagine, what we think,
what seems to be so and, on the other hand,
what is so.

However, though these three compo-
nents all function in the objectivity of adult
human knowing, still it is one thing for
them to function and it is quite another to
become explicitly aware that they function.
Such explicit awareness presupposes that
one is not a truncated subject, aware indeed of his sensations and his speech, but
aware of little more than that. Then, what
is meant by "object" and "objective," is
something to be settled not by any scrutiny
of one's operations and their properties, but
by picture-thinking. An object, for picture-
thinking, has to be something one looks at;
knowing it has to be something like look-

ing, peering, seeing, intuiting, perceiving;
and objectivity, finally, has to be a matter
of seeing all that is there to be seen and
nothing that is not there.

Once picture-thinking takes over, immanence is an inevitable consequence.[6]
What is intended in questioning, is not
seen, intuited, perceived; it is as yet unknown; it is what we do not know but seek
to know. It follows that the intention of
questioning, the notion of being, is merely
immanent, merely subjective. Again, what
is grasped in understanding, is not some
further datum added on to the data of sense
and of consciousness; on the contrary, it
is quite unlike all data; it consists in an intelligible unity or pattern that is, not perceived, but understood; and it is understood, not as necessarily relevant to the
data, but only as possibly relevant. Now
the grasp of something that is possibly relevant is nothing like seeing, intuiting, perceiving, which regard only what is actually
there. It follows that, for picture-thinking,
understanding too must be merely immanent and merely subjective. What holds

for understanding, also holds for concepts, for concepts express what has been grasped by understanding. What holds for concepts, holds no less for judgments, since judgments proceed from a reflective understanding, just as concepts proceed from a direct or inverse understanding.

This conclusion of immanence is inevitable, once picture-thinking is admitted. For picture-thinking means thinking in visual images. Visual images are incapable of representing or suggesting the normative exigences of intelligence and reasonableness and, much less, their power to effect the intentional self-transcendence of the subject.

The foregoing account, however, though it provides the key to doctrines of immanence, provides no more than a key. It is a general model based on knowledge of the subject. It differs from actual doctrines of immanence, inasmuch as the latter are the work of truncated subjects that have only a partial apprehension of their own reality. But it requires, I think, no great discernment to find a parallel between the foregoing account and, to take but a single example, the Kantian argument for immanence. In this argument the effective distinction is between immediate and mediate relations of cognitional activities to objects. Judgment is only a mediate knowledge of objects, a representation of a representation.[7] Reason is never related right up to objects but only to understanding and, through understanding, to the empirical use of reason itself.[8]

Since our only cognitional activity immediately related to objects is intuition,[9] it follows that the value of our judgments and our reasoning can be no more than the value of our intuitions. But our only intuitions are sensitive; sensitive intuitions reveal not being but phenomena; and so our judgments and reasoning are confined to a merely phenomenal world.[10]

Such, substantially, seems to be the Kantian argument. It is a quite valid argument if one means by "object" what one can settle by picture-thinking. "Object" is what one looks at; looking is sensitive intuition; it alone is immediately related to objects; understanding and reason can be related to objects only mediately, only through sensitive intuition.

Moreover, the neglected and truncated subject is not going to find the answer to Kant, for he does not know himself well enough to break the hold of picture-thinking and to discover that human cognitional activities have as their object being, that the activity immediately related to this object is questioning, that other activities such as sense and consciousness, understanding and judgment, are related mediately to the object, being, inasmuch as they are the means of answering questions, of reaching the goal intended by questioning.

There is a final point to be made. The transition from the neglected and truncated subject to self-appropriation is not a simple matter. It is not just a matter of finding out and assenting to a number of true propositions. More basically, it is a matter of conversion, of a personal philosophic experience, of moving out of a world of sense and of arriving, dazed and disorientated for a while, into a universe of being.

The Existential Subject

So far, our reflections on the subject have been concerned with him as a knower, as one that experiences, understands, and judges. We have now to think of him as a doer, as one that deliberates, evaluates, chooses, acts. Such doing, at first sight, affects, modifies, changes the world of objects. But even more it affects the subject himself. For human doing is free and responsible. Within it is contained the reality of morals, of building up or destroying character, of achieving personality or failing in that task. By his own acts the human subject makes himself what he is to be, and he does so freely and responsibly; indeed, he does so precisely because his acts are the free and responsible expressions of himself.

Such is the existential subject. It is a notion that is overlooked on the schematism of older categories that distinguished faculties, such as intellect and will, or different uses of the same faculty, such as speculative and practical intellect, or different types of human activity, such as theoretical

inquiry and practical execution. None of
these distinctions adverts to the subject as
such and, while the reflexive, self-constitu-
tive element in moral living has been known
from ancient times, still it was not coupled
with the notion of the subject to draw attention to him in his key role of making
himself what he is to be.

Because the older schemes are not relevant, it will aid clarity if I indicate the new
scheme of distinct but related levels of consciousness, in which the existential subject
stands, so to speak, on the top level. For we
are subjects, as it were, by degrees. At a
lowest level, when unconscious in dream-
less sleep or in a coma, we are merely po-
tentially subjects. Next, we have a minimal degree of consciousness and subjecti-
vity when we are the helpless subjects of
our dreams. Thirdly, we become experiential subjects when we awake, when we become the subjects of lucid perception, im-
aginative projects, emotional and conative
impulses, and bodily action. Fourthly, the
intelligent subject sublates the experiential, i.e., it retains, preserves, goes beyond,

completes it, when we inquire about our experience, investigate, grow in understanding, express our inventions and discoveries.
Fifthly, the rational subject sublates the
intelligent and experiential subject, when
we question our own understanding, check
our formulations and expressions, ask
whether we have got things right, marshal
the evidence *pro* and *con,* judge this to be
so and that not to be so. Sixthly, finally,
rational consciousness is sublated by rational self-consciousness, when we deliber-
ate, evaluate, decide, act. Then there
emerges human consciousness at its fullest.
Then the existential subject exists and his
character, his personal essence, is at stake.

The levels of consciousness are not only
distinct but also related, and the relations
are best expressed as instances of what
Hegel named sublation, of a lower being
retained, preserved, yet transcended and
completed by a higher.[11] Human intelligence goes beyond human sensitivity yet
it cannot get along without sensitivity. Human judgment goes beyond sensitivity and
intelligence yet cannot function except in

conjunction with them. Human action, finally, must in similar fashion both presuppose and complete human sensitivity, intelligence, and judgment.

It is, of course, this fact of successive sublations that is denoted by the metaphor of levels of consciousness. But besides their distinction and their functional interdependence, the levels of consciousness are united by the unfolding of a single transcendental intending of plural, interchangeable objectives.[12] What promotes the subject from experiential to intellectual consciousness is the desire to understand, the intention of intelligibility. What next promotes him from intellectual to rational consciousness, is a fuller unfolding of the same intention: for the desire to understand, once understanding is reached, becomes the desire to understand correctly; in other words, the intention of intelligibility, once an intelligible is reached, becomes the intention of the right intelligible, of the true and, through truth, of reality. Finally, the intention of the intelligible, the true, the real, becomes also the intention of the good, the question of value, of what is worth while, when the already acting subject confronts his world and adverts to his own acting in it.

I am suggesting that the transcendental notion of the good regards value. It is distinct from the particular good that satisfies individual appetite, such as the appetite for food and drink, the appetite for union and communion, the appetite for knowledge, or virtue, or pleasure. Again, it is distinct from the good of order, the objective arrangement or institution that ensures for a group of people the regular recurrence of particular goods. As appetite wants breakfast, so an economic system is to ensure breakfast every morning. As appetite wants union, so marriage is to ensure life-long union. As appetite wants knowledge, so an educational system ensures the imparting of knowledge to each successive generation. But beyond the particular good and the good of order, there is the good of value. It is by appealing to value or values that we satisfy some appetites and do not satisfy others, that we approve some systems for achieving the good of order and disapprove of others, that we praise or blame human persons as good or evil and their actions as right or wrong.

What, then, is value? I should say that it is a transcendental notion like the notion of being. Just as the notion of being intends but, of itself, does not know being, so too the notion of value intends but, of itself, does not know value. Again, as the notion of being is the dynamic principle that keeps us moving toward ever fuller knowledge of being, so the notion of value is the fuller flowering of the same dynamic principle that now keeps us moving toward ever fuller realization of the good, of what is worth while.

This may seem nebulous, so I beg leave to introduce a parallel. There is to Aristotle's *Ethics* an empiricism that seems almost question-begging. He could write: "Actions . . . are called just and temperate when they are such as the just or the temperate man would do; but it is not the man who does these that is just and temperate, but the man who also does them *as* just

and temperate men do them."[13] Again, he
could add: "Virtue ... is a state of character
concerned with choice, lying in a mean, i.e.
the mean relative to us, this being deter-
mined by a rational principle, and by that
principle by which the man of practical
wisdom would determine it."[14] Aristotle, it
seems to me, is refusing to speak of ethics
apart from the ethical reality of good men,
of justice apart from men that are just, of
temperance apart from men that are temperate, of the nature of virtue apart from
the judgment of the man that possesses
practical wisdom.

But, whatever may be the verdict about
Aristotle, at least the approach I have just
noted fits in admirably with the notion of
the good I am outlining. Just as the notion
of being functions in one's knowing and it
is by reflecting on that functioning that one
comes to know what the notion of being is,
so also the notion or intention of the good
functions within one's human acting and it
is by reflection on that functioning that one
comes to know what the notion of good is.
Again, just as the functioning of the notion

of being brings about our limited knowledge of being, so too the functioning of the notion of the good brings about our limited achievement of the good. Finally, as our knowledge of being is, not knowledge of essence, but only knowledge of this and that and other beings, so too the only good, to which we have first-hand access, is found in instances of the good realized in themselves or produced beyond themselves by good men.

So the paradox of the existential subject extends to the good existential subject. Just as the existential subject freely and responsibly makes himself what he is, so too he makes himself good or evil and his actions right or wrong. The good subject, the good choice, the good action are not found in isolation. For the subject is good by his good choices and good actions. Universally prior to any choice or action there is just the transcendental principle of all appraisal and criticism, the intention of the good. That principle gives rise to instances of the good, but those instances are good choices and actions. However, do not ask me to determine them, for their determination in each case is the work of the free and responsible subject producing the first and only edition of himself.

It is because the determination of the good is the work of freedom that ethical systems can catalogue sins in almost endless genera and species yet always remain rather vague about the good. They urge us to do good as well as to avoid evil, but what it is to do good does not get much beyond the golden rule, the precept of universal charity, and the like. Still the short-comings of system are not an irremediable defect. We come to know the good from the example of those about us, from the stories people tell of the good and evil men and women of old, from the incessant flow of praise and blame that makes up the great part of human conversation, from the elation and from the shame that fill us when our own choices and deeds are our own determination of ourselves as good or evil, praiseworthy or blameworthy.

I have been affirming a primacy of the existential. I distinguished different levels

of human consciousness to place rational
self-consciousness at the top. It sublates the
three prior levels of experiencing, of understanding, and of judging, where, of course,
sublating means not destroying, not inter-
fering, but retaining, preserving, going beyond, perfecting. The experiential, the intelligible, the true, the real, the good are
one, so that understanding enlightens experience, truth is the correctness of understanding, and the pursuit of the good, of
value, of what is worth while in no way
conflicts with, in every way promotes and
completes, the pursuit of the intelligible,
the true, the real.

It is to be noted, however, that we are
not speaking of the good in the Aristotelian
sense of the object of appetite, *id quod
omnia appetunt.* Nor are we speaking of
the good in the intellectual and, indeed,
Thomist sense of the good of order. Besides these there is a quite distinct meaning of the word, good; to it we refer specifically when we speak of value, of what is
worth while, of what is right as opposed to
wrong, of what is good as opposed not to

bad but to evil. It is the intention of the
good in this sense that prolongs the intention of the intelligible, the true, the real,
that founds rational self-consciousness, that
constitutes the emergence of the existential
subject.

Finally, let me briefly say that the primacy of the existential does not mean the
primacy of results, as in pragmatism, or
the primacy of will, as a Scotist might urge,
or a primacy of practical intellect, or practical reason, as an Aristotelian or Kantian
might phrase it. Results proceed from
actions, actions from decisions, decisions
from evaluations, evaluations from deliber-
ations, and all five from the existential subject, the subject as deliberating, evaluating,
deciding, acting, bringing about results.
That subject is not just an intellect or just
a will. Though concerned with results, he
or she more basically is concerned with
himself or herself as becoming good or evil
and so is to be named, not a practical subject, but an existential subject.

The Alienated Subject

Existential reflection is at once enlightening and enriching. Not only does it touch us intimately and speak to us convincingly but also it is the natural starting-point for fuller reflection on the subject as incarnate, as image and feeling as well as mind and will, as moved by symbol and story, as intersubjective, as encountering others and becoming "I" to "Thou" to move on to "We" through acquaintance, companionship, collaboration, friendship, love. Then easily we pass into the whole human world founded on meaning, a world of language, art, literature, science, philosophy, history, of family and mores, society and education, state and law, economy and technology. That human world does not come into being or survive without deliberation, evaluation, decision, action, without the exercise of freedom and responsibility. It is a world of existential subjects and it objectifies the values that they originate in their creativity and their freedom.

But the very wealth of existential reflection can turn out to be a trap. It is indeed the key that opens the doors to a philosophy, not of man in the abstract, but of concrete human living in its historical unfolding. Still, one must not think that such concreteness eliminates the ancient problems of cognitional theory, epistemology, and metaphysics, for if they occur in an abstract context, they recur with all the more force in a concrete context.

Existential reflection, as it reveals what it is for man to be good, so it raises the question whether the world is good. Is this whole process from the nebulae through plants and animals to man, is it good, a true value, something worth while? This question can be answered affirmatively, if and only if one acknowledges God's existence, his omnipotence, and his goodness. Granted those three, one can say that created process is good because the creative *fiat* cannot but be good. Doubt or deny any of the three, and then one doubts or denies any intelligent mind and loving will that could justify anyone saying that this world is good, worth while, a value worthy of man's approval and consent. For "good" in the sense we have been using the term is the goodness of the moral agent, his deeds, his works. Unless there is a moral agent responsible for the world's being and becoming, the world cannot be said to be good in that moral sense. If in that sense the world is not good, then goodness in that sense is to be found only in man. If still man would be good, he is alien to the rest of the universe. If on the other hand he renounces authentic living and drifts into the now seductive and now harsh rhythms of his psyche and of nature, then man is alienated from himself.

It is, then, no accident that a theatre of the absurd, a literature of the absurd, and philosophies of the absurd flourish in a culture in which there are theologians to proclaim that God is dead. But that absurdity and that death have their roots in a new neglect of the subject, a new truncation, a new immanentism. In the name of phenomenology, of existential self-understanding, of human encounter, of salvation history, there are those that resentfully and disdainfully brush aside the old questions of cognitional theory, epistemology, meta-physics. I have no doubt, I never did doubt, that the old answers were defective. But to reject the questions as well is to refuse to know what one is doing when one is know-ing; it is to refuse to know why doing that is knowing; it is to refuse to set up a basic semantics by concluding what one knows when one does it. That threefold refusal is worse than mere neglect of the subject, and it generates a far more radical truncation. It is that truncation that we experience to-day not only without but within the Church, when we find that the conditions of the possibility of significant dialogue are not grasped, when the distinction between revealed religion and myth is blurred, when the possibility of objective knowledge of God's existence and of his goodness is denied.

These are large and urgent topics. I shall not treat them. Yet I do not think I am neglecting them entirely, for I have pointed throughout this paper to the root difficulty, to neglect of the subject and the vast labor involved in knowing him.

NOTES

1. One should, perhaps, start from Kant's Coperni-
   can revolution, which brought the subject into
   technical prominence while making only minimal
   concessions to its reality. The subsequent movement then appears as a series of attempts to win
   for the subject acknowledgement of its full reality
   and its functions. For a careful survey of the
   movement and its ambiguities, see James Brown,
   Subject and Object in Modern Theology, New
   York: Macmillan, 1955.

2. The formally unconditioned has no conditions
   whatever; it is God. The virtually unconditioned
   has conditions but they have been fulfilled. Such,
   I should say, is the cognitional counterpart of
   contingent being and, as well, a technical formu-
   lation of the ordinary criterion of true judgment,
   namely, sufficient evidence. See my book, *Insight,*
   London: Longmans, 1957, chapter ten, for more
   details.

3. See H. Lennerz, *De Virtutibus Theologicis,*
   Rome: Gregorian Press, 1947, pp. 98 f., 103,
   #196, 204. L. Billot, *De Virtutibus Infusis,*
   Rome: Gregorian Press, 1928, pp. 191 ff., 313.

4. For a contrast of Aristotle and Augustine and
   their relations to Aquinas, see the Introduction
   in my *Verbum, Word and Idea in Aquinas,* Notre
   Dame: Notre Dame University Press, 1967. The
   same material appeared also in *Philippine Studies,*
   13 (1965) 576-585, under the title "Subject and
   Soul."

5. For a fuller statement, *Insight,* chapter thirteen,
   and for something more compendious, *Collection,*
   New York: Herder and Herder, 1967, pp. 227-
   231.

6. Provided, of course, one's account of human

intellect is not more picture-thinking, with human intelligence a matter of looking.

7.   I. Kant, *Kritik der reinen Vernunft,* A 68, B 93.
8.   *Ibid.,* A 643, B 671.
9.   *Ibid.,* A 19, B 33.
10. See F. Copleston, *A History of Philosophy,* 8 vols., Glen Rock: Newman Press, 1946-, Vol. 6, chapter 12, #1 and 8. Paperback (Image Books, Doubleday) VI-2, pp. 30 ff., 60 ff. Contrast with E. Gilson and E. Coreth in *Collection,* pp. 202-220.
11. This omits, however, the Hegelian view that the higher reconciles a contradiction in the lower.
12. These objectives are approximately the Scholastic transcendentals, *ens, unum, verum, bonum,* and they are interchangeable in the sense of mutual predication, of *convertuntur.*
13. Aristotle, *Nicomachean Ethics,* II, iii, 4; 1105b 5-8.
14. *Ibid.,* II, vi, 15; 1106b 36 f. Translations by W. D. Ross in R. McKeon's *Basic Works of Aristotle,* New York: Random House, 1941, pp. 956, 959.

Published by the Marquette University Press
Milwaukee, Wisconsin 53233
United States of America

#1 St. Thomas and the Life of Learning (1937)
by John F. McCormick, S.J. (1874-1943)
professor of philosophy, Loyola University.
ISBN 0-87462-101-1

#2 St. Thomas and the Gentiles (1938) by Morti-
mer J. Adler, Ph.D., Director of the Institute of Philosophical Research, San Francisco,
Calif.   ISBN 0-87462-102-X

#3 St. Thomas and the Greeks (1939) by Anton
C. Pegis, Ph.D., professor of philosophy,
Pontifical Institute of Mediaeval Studies,
Toronto.   ISBN 0-87462-103-8

#4 The Nature and Functions of Authority (1940)
by Yves Simon, Ph.D., (1903-1961) professor of philosophy of social thought, University of Chicago.   ISBN 0-87462-104-6

#5 St. Thomas and Analogy (1941) by Gerald B.
Phelan, Ph.D., (1892-1965) professor of phi-
losophy, St. Michael's College, Toronto.
ISBN 0-87462-105-4

#6 St. Thomas and the Problem of Evil (1942) by
Jacques Maritain, Ph.D., professor *emeritus*
of philosophy, Princeton University.
ISBN 0-87462-106-2

#7 Humanism and Theology (1943) by Werner
Jaeger, Ph.D., Litt.D., (1888-1961) Univer-
sity professor, Harvard University.
ISBN 0-87462-107-0

#42 The Catholic University and the Faith (1978) by Francis C. Wade, S.J., professor of philosophy, Marquette University.
ISBN 0-87462-143-7

#43 St. Thomas and Historicity (1979) by Armand Maurer, C.S.B., professor of philosophy, University of Toronto and the Pontifical Institute of Mediaeval Studies, Toronto.
ISBN 0-87462-144-5

#44 Does God Have a Nature? (1980) by Alvin Plantinga, Ph.D., professor of philosophy, Calvin College, Grand Rapids, Michigan.
ISBN 0-87462-145-3

#45 Rhyme and Reason: St. Thomas and Modes of Discourse (1981) by Ralph McInerny, Ph.D., professor of Medieval Studies, University of Notre Dame. ISBN 0-87462-148-8

Uniform format, cover and binding.

Copies of this Aquinas Lecture and the others in the series are obtainable from:

Marquette University Press
Marquette University
Milwaukee, Wisconsin 53233, U.S.A.